OUR FRIENDS FROM THE UNITED STATES, CANADA, AND BEYOND

A TRIBUTE

by

OSWALD "OZZIE" TYSON

To Pamella
Ozzie Tyson
march 15 - 2015

ISBN-13: 978-1500740573

ISBN-10:1500740578

NOTE TO THE READER

I am well aware that there have been countless visitors to Nevis who have made important contributions to the welfare of our Island over the years. In the text which follows, I limit my comments to mention of those folks I have known personally or whom I have come to know about via my contacts with friends and associates.

I am certain that even those well-deserving folks whom I have singled out for praise have done much more than I have reported. Therefore, I sincerely hope that readers will understand the spirit which motivates this tribute and not be distracted by its shortcomings.

Author's Preface

Recently, I remembered that back in 1969, when the US Apollo mission went to the Moon, there was a local lady named Mrs. Taylor who was in her late eighties. Soon after the Moon landing, we had more than ten inches of rainfall on Nevis. Mrs. Taylor said, "Lord, dey went go trouble de Moon and de Moon a leak." I was a boy at that time, but I found that very funny. She thought the Moon was made of ice and if you walked on it, it would break up and start to melt. I tried to explain to her that the Moon is not like that, but I could not change her mind.

Mrs. Taylor was a good woman, a hard-working woman who farmed a plot of land on the Clarke Estate for some seventy years. She was nearly a hundred years old when she died, probably still believing that the Americans had caused her crops to be drenched.

Remembering that story made me think of how many people I have met who have the wrong idea about Americans. I knew long ago that the Americans did not make the Moon rain on Nevis. Now, many years later, I also know that our American visitors, as well as those from many other countries, deserve our thanks and not our criticism. That is why I have written this tribute, to express our gratitude and to share my experiences with my countrymen at home and abroad so that all may join me in saying thank you.

From the time of Alexander Hamilton down to today, many Nevisians have looked to the United States as a place where they could go, be successful, and better themselves and their families. I remember a man named Bertram Baker who left Nevis as a young man and traveled to New York in search of a better life. He was born on Nevis in 1898 and left for the US at age seventeen.

Young Baker obtained a job as a bookkeeper, and, in time, he became head of the Accounting Division of Cox and Nostrand. Later he started his own accounting business and was subsequently appointed as Deputy Collector for the US Internal Revenue Service.

Mr. Baker joined the Democratic Party in 1930, and in 1948, he became the first black man to be elected to the New York State Legislature. Working his way up in the Party, he was elected Majority Whip in the New York House of Representatives.

He was a founding member of the National Black Tennis Association paving the way for world champions Althea Gibson and Arthur Ashe. His granddaughter, Diane, is the First Lady of Massachusetts being the wife of the Commonwealth's current Governor, Duval Patrick.

This is just one of the many success stories of Nevisians who worked hard and benefited from the opportunities they found by following their dreams.

Mr. Baker left Nevis a long time ago. Today, many more young people can find their future here on the Island thanks to the investments made by our visitors from abroad--not just from the US, but also from Canada, from England, from Europe, from Asia, from Africa.

Before these investors from overseas arrived, Nevisians had to struggle to survive. Many folks had little or no cash income. There was no social security and no pensions. Relief for the Poor came to some US 40 cents every other week. Old people, like Mrs. Taylor, had to work long hours well into their Golden Age to make ends meet. Today, Nevis is a very different place. Our visitors have brought prosperity to our beautiful island. We are grateful to them and we wish them and their countries well.

I know that our visitors care deeply about our island. That is why they come back, year after year. That is why they pump millions of dollars into our economy. That is why so many of them volunteer to help with projects all over the island. That is why they bring us many gifts. I know I am speaking for many of my countrymen and women when I say, "Thank you!"

Oswald "Ozzie" Tyson - February 2014

DEDICATION

I dedicate this Tribute to the following persons who have made major contributions to the betterment of Nevis

- ❖ The late Marvin and Lou Anderson

- ❖ David Robinson

- ❖ The late Joan Robinson

- ❖ Donald and Paula Flemming

- ❖ Amba Trott

- ❖ David and Marsha Myers

- ❖ The late Jack and Jessie Williams

- ❖ The late John and Thelma Miller

- ❖ The late Vincent Hubbard

- ❖ Bill and Stella Nokes

ACKNOWLEDGMENTS

Special thanks to Donald and Paula Flemming. Without them, I would not be able to tell the world what's on my mind. I thank them for their hard work and the time spent helping me to make this Tribute possible. They are a great American family including their son Sean, who is a kind American citizen. I thank you all for all you have done to help me and for your contributions to Nevis. God bless you all!

While the Flemmings have helped me with editing and preparation for publication, I am solely responsible for the content. I have tried to report the facts as I know them, but I apologize in advance for any errors of omission or commission.

It was the visitors from abroad who started to develop Nevis from a sugar and agricultural economy to a service economy. I feel moved to write about some of them many of whom I have met starting as a young child though many have long since gone to the Great Beyond.

Some of our early visitors from abroad were Jewish settlers who at one time had a thriving community on Nevis. There are still some remnants of their presence here such as the Jewish cemetery on Government Road and remains of their synagogue not far away. But many Nevisians do not know that there is part of an old synagogue on the Tower Hill Estate. There is also an old cemetery way up there as well as the ruin of a Great House. Some people in the villages of Cotton Ground and Barnes Ghaut know about the ruins. They know that some of the early Jewish colony lived on what became the Tower Hill Estate and left their mark there.

You might wonder why I know about that place way up on Mt. Nevis that many people have never heard of. Well, as a boy, I knew there were lots of lime and sour orange trees on Tower Hill Estate. I used to go up there with the older boys to look for limes and sour oranges to put in my sack and bring home.

The next day I would take the sailboat (lighter) over to St. Kitts to sell the fruit and use whatever money I could get to buy groceries for my Mom at the supermarket. Many other youngsters did the same thing. We were all very poor and we knew our mothers had a hard time getting money for food. So we did what we could to help.

That is how I stumbled upon the cemetery on Tower Hill. Also, a number of local men used to go up there to make moonshine, a drink we call hammond or bush rum. They knew the police would destroy the operation if they found it and arrest anyone they caught boiling and take them down to jail. Some say they would drink the bush rum they confiscated. So the men would go far up the hill to make their moonshine. That's how the old boys knew about the ruins. Sadly, many of the moonshine men are no longer with us.

The Tower Hill Estate is quite a mystery. There were two old ladies in Cotton Ground Village, distant relatives of mine. Their names were Rhoda and Carol. When I knew the ladies, they were in their late eighties, close to ninety. Rhoda didn't have any children, but Carol had one daughter.

One Sunday, one of my Great Aunts and I went to visit the ladies. We lived at the end of the village, and they lived about a quarter mile up the hill in a large wooden house much bigger than the average house in those days with lots of fruit trees in the garden. We sat down in the living room and the old ladies told us a story.

Many years before, when they were teenagers, their mother and father were both farmers who worked on a farm way up on Tower Hill. The summer was very dry but there was an old cistern not too far away even though the house was not in livable condition. The cistern had a lot of water so they obeyed their parents and got a rope that was made from the bark of a tree. It was good water. They filled their buckets.

When they were about to leave, they heard the voice of a lady saying to them, "That water is mine, this cistern is mine, take your buckets and go and don't come back!" Looking through the bushes was a blond lady dressed in pure white. But she was a ghost!

They dropped their buckets and ran all the way to Cotton Ground and never went back to that place again. And that's the story they told me many years ago.

In the early 1600's when the Spanish traveled to these islands, they brought some treasure to Nevis. Or so I was told by the older folks on the Island who had heard the story from their ancestors. A man named Phil Miller came to Nevis in the late 1960's to manage the Cliff Dwellers Hotel. Phil was a great chef whose favorite dish was a steak and lobster bake. Phil, a devoted husband and father, had a wife named Judy and two young children, Kelly and Septemberly. They were well-behaved and good-mannered children who attended the St. Thomas School which at the time was all ages.

My job was to take care of them at school since I was a little older than them and in a higher grade. They were quite fond of my family. My brother Alex and I often got odd jobs from the Millers, and sometimes we babysat the children.

Mr. Miller was fond of old stories as well as treasure hunting. I don't know who told him about the "90 man war". That was the place where the old people say there is hidden treasure. Phil decided that he would try to find it.

The place is said to be haunted by the spirits of the old soldiers who died there. They are standing guard to protect the treasure which is said to be gold coins inside of two small iron coppers, one bolted on top of the other.

There was a man from the village of Westbury who went one time to cut wood in that location when suddenly the treasure appeared before him. He was afraid to touch it, so he ran home and told his wife what he had seen. Then he called some friends to help him, but when they reached the place he had seen it, the treasure had disappeared. They searched all over but couldn't find it. It seems that the spirits or ghosts had wanted to give the treasure to him alone so that they could rest from having to watch over the treasure for four centuries.

After that, no one ventured to the spot looking for the treasure. That is, until Mr. Miller heard all the old stories about gold being hidden away in the hills of Nevis at a place called "90 man war". He decided that he would get a few of his employees to accompany him to that place along with the company earth mover. So off they went to get the gold.

When they arrived at the spot, Phil started digging up the soil with his bulldozer. Suddenly, a herd of bone hogs started coming towards him. The huge hogs didn't seem at all afraid of the bulldozer. Phil and his group realized that they were not pigs but ghosts appearing to be pigs. They were approaching with such a force that Mr. Miller and his party left the machine and ran down the hill toward the Main Road.

As much as Mr. Miller loved treasure hunting, he never returned to try to find the treasure. Almost a year passed before someone went to get the bulldozer from "90 man war". In 1972, the Millers returned to the US so that their children could continue their education there.

Mr. Wells McCormack came to Nevis in the early 1960's and bought more than two hundred acres in the Jones Estate. He started building the once famous Cliff Dwellers Hotel which opened its doors in the winter of 1965. The Hotel was built on a hill, and most of the guests had to go up and down the hill in a cable car. It had stops close to each guest room. Mr. McCormack also built a road that year. You could have driven a car or a truck on the back road, but most taxi drivers never wanted to drive up that road as it was very steep.

I worked at that Hotel as a young man. When the cable car wasn't working, all of the bartenders had to walk down to the bottom of the hill--over 250 feet--to bring the guests' luggage to the top. It was very hard work, but when you got a tip, you felt very rewarded.

There was a staff of more than thirty people for a small, fourteen room hotel. The place was jumping! Every Sunday there was a pool party, a donkey race and a crab race. People from all over Nevis had a nice place to go on Sundays. The Sunday special was lobster served with butter and garlic sauce and lime wedges. There was also roast suckling pig and curried goat made with coconut milk. The curry was served with white rice and the roast pig with potato salad and freshly picked tomatoes.

The Cliff Dwellers Hotel had its own garden. A man named Harry Cole was in charge of that department. The Greenes, Stuart and his wife, Gerry, were the managers. A great job they did! Mr. & Mrs. Greene treated their staff well. They were from Canada, and Mr. Bond, Mr. McCormack's project manager was an American from Florida.

Well, Mr. Greene was fond of sailing. One weekend, he and a young man named Skeete (most people called him Congo) went out for a sail. As they were nearing shore, the boat exploded. Skeete threw Mr.Greene to safety but he, himself, lost his life. He was totally burned leaving a girlfriend and lots of children behind. Mr. Greene was devastated that his employee and friend gave up his life to save him.

Mr. & Mrs. Greene returned to Canada the next year, but that was not the end of the Greenes. They built a house in the village we call Newcastle, and every year they came back to Nevis for a few weeks. When the Greenes retired, they spent winters on Nevis. As they advanced in years, they sold the house, but they still visited Nevis from time to time. Mr. Greene died some fourteen years ago.

Mr. McCormack not only built the Cliff Dwellers Hotel, he also started a construction company. Mr. Bond, his Project Manager, was also a good contractor who developed Jones Estate. Mr. McCormack sold land by house lots of an acre and a half and a few of two acres. Mr. Bond built many homes in Jones Estate. Most are still intact. Some have changed hands many times over the past forty-six years.

In 1965, Rick Parker from the East coast of the US--now a resident of Florida--came to Nevis and did some work for Mr. McCormack's assistant, Mr. Bond. Mr. Bond was fond of a hard worker named Joshua. When Bond returned to Florida, he sent for Joshua to come and work for him. Joshua left Nevis for Florida and worked for Mr. Bond until Joshua died some ten years ago. If Mr. Bond is still living, he has to be near a hundred.

Bond was a much older man than Mr. Parker who is now in his mid-eighties. Rick, as we called Mr. Parker, was quite the builder at forty years of age. All the homes he built in the sixties are still in good condition. They have withstood many hurricanes.

In the early 70's, Mr. McCormack leased the then Cliff Dwellers Hotel to a guy from the US named Frank. Well, Mr. Frank, as we knew him, ran the hotel for two years. The last managers who worked for Mr. Frank were Scott McDonald and his wife. They were a lovely couple and they loved me. They even gave me a room in the hotel. It was a great time for me.

After that time, Mr. Frank gave the hotel back to Mr. McCormack who decided he'd had enough and never opened the hotel again. As a result, many people were out of work including me. Even though I was very young, I had been employed as a bartender at the hotel.

I started working at Cliff Dwellers when Mr. & Mrs. Cory were managers. I was too young to work at the bar then, so I worked raking up leaves and washing cars for two dollars.

Ira Martin was Assistant Manager but he filled in as Manager for many, many years until he left Nevis.

Late in 1975, Mr. McCormack passed away. Mrs. McCormack and her children were not interested in running the hotel. It remained closed for five years until David and Marsha Myers bought Cliff Dwellers. They opened the hotel in the fall of 1978. It was great to see the hotel open once again. Many Nevisians started working there. I worked with the Myers until the hotel was destroyed by Hurricane Hugo in 1989.

Mrs. Myers is still a part of Cliff Dwellers after all these years. She and a business partner have developed condos on the Cliff Dweller's property. So, the Jones Estate property was initially developed by the Americans and many Americans own the houses and condos which have been built there.

But we have had many visitors from other lands as well. Mr. James Gaskell came to Nevis from England as a young lawyer. He bought the Montpelier Estate and turned the Plantation into one of the best plantation inns anywhere. It was truly fit for a princess so when the late Princess Diana visited Nevis, she and her boys stayed at Montpelier.

Not only did Gaskell turn the property into a hotel, he created long-term employment for several Nevisians. The Gaskells are no longer in the hotel business. Montpelier is now owned by the Hoffman family. They are from the US. Montpelier serves one of the best meals on Nevis.

The hotel has luxurious rooms with a beautiful view of our sister island, St. Kitts.

Mrs. Margaret Lyman and her husband of Houston, Texas, came to Nevis in the 70's and bought a house in Jones Estate. Not long after, she and her best friend, who was also her business partner, started the Fun Day event. Once a year those ladies would get other people to join them in what we call a jumble sale. Those ladies called it a Fun Fair. They would collect donations of clothes and sell them to folks who attended the Fair. The money raised would go to buy equipment for the Alexandra Hospital and the infirmary, a home for the aged.

Mrs. Lyman--folks called her Peggy--and her husband ran a store in Charlestown, the capital of Nevis. Although Harry Lyman died in 1986, Peggy kept her house as long as she could.

When she was in her eighties, she sold it to a young American family, but every year she would come with her friend for a stay on Nevis. Mrs. Lyman died in Texas a few years ago at a ripe old age--she was in her nineties! But her spirit lives on with us as she did so much for the island of Nevis.

Ned and Shirley Mullen came to Nevis in the sixties. Mr. Mullen was a PanAm pilot who decided to retire on this island. His wife did a lot of charity work on Nevis to help the disabled and those who didn't know where their next meal was coming from. I recall that she used to bring food to a local lady named Mrs. Henry.

Mr. Mullen wanted to live out his sunset years on Nevis, but it was not to be. Because of ill health, the Mullens sold their house and moved back to the States where Mr. Mullen died in his sixties, still a young man. They had so much to offer, but God knows best.

John and Thelma Miller came to Nevis in the early 1960's on vacation. They stayed at the Cliff Dwellers Hotel—the place to be at the time. They loved Nevis so they bought some land from Wells McCormack and built a lovely home. The Millers had three sons who would come to visit them on Nevis from time to time.

Mr. Miller and his wife were devoted Roman Catholics who loved to support anything the Church was doing. Mr. Miller helped with the Church's fund-raising efforts and on Sundays he would take part in the service by reading from the Scriptures. The Millers would give up their time to help out our senior citizens and they also gave generously to the poor on the Island.

John Miller passed away some twenty-four years ago with Thelma at his side. He was buried in Bath Cemetery. Mrs. Miller kept the house for many years after her husband died, but, as the house was large, she decided to sell that house and build a smaller one not far from her first home. After many years of doing good work to help folks on Nevis, Thelma passed away leaving her house to her younger son, Scott. He and his wife and children share their parents' love for Nevis.

Mr. & Mrs. Ferguson built their house on Nevis in the mid-sixties. Mrs. Ferguson was fond of animals.

She started to raise milking goats on Nevis, and she did a great job. She would milk her goats and give the milk to some of our school children whose parents were having a very hard time of it. In those days, many people, myself included, could not afford to buy the basic necessities. So when Liz, as we affectionately called her, provided milk for many grade school children, it was a great thing.

Mrs. Ferguson came to Nevis from November to the end of April. She left her hired help to take care of her goats until she returned when she would care for them once again. There was an elderly gentleman named Mr. Wilkerson whom she left to take care of the goats. She told him, "You must milk the goats daily and give the milk to the schools". But he never milked the goats. So when Mrs. Ferguson returned, she asked him, "Did you do what I told you to do?" He said, "Madam, I left them up to nature!" Mrs. Ferguson told him he was fired for not taking proper care of her goats.

The Fergusons were a great American family who loved Nevis. After they got on in years, they sold their property and moved back to the US. I worked for the Fergusons' daughter, Ann, along with two of my older brothers when I was a child.

There was a family named Jones, Elijah and Jane, who had bought property on Nevis. Mr. Jones' love of golf led him to build the first golf course on Nevis. It is still in service today, used by the men and women members of the Nevis Golf Association. Membership is open to everyone on the island.

The Joneses are no longer with us. Jane Jones passed away back in Canada. Her husband, El, died about seven years ago. He and the late John F. Kennedy were in the service together. Mr. Jones' son, Michael, still owns the property on Nevis which he inherited when his parents passed away.

Another great American family were the Gotshalls. George and Maryann. They were great company to be with. The Gotshalls came from Michigan. They built a house near Cliff Dwellers on the beach side. George was a lawyer back in Michigan, and so were most of his friends who came down.

His wife was one of the best persons you will find on this Earth. She was very kind and cared for the poor people on Nevis. She and George worked hard over the years to raise funds to help the hospital and the Poor House, as it was called back in those days. They were helped by Paul Peter and his wife, Mitchell, along with Dick Ames and his wife.

The Gotshalls sold their home to the Yancys in the eighties, a few years before George passed away back in Michigan.

Also from Michigan were Mr. & Mrs. Verdier. Mr. Verdier was also a lawyer and a golfer. His wife, Anita, was a loving and kind person who would come to my village of Cotton Ground and do what she could to help with the children who didn't have books and pencils for school. Mrs. Verdier was a lady who had a great love for the poor people of Nevis.

She was very concerned that the young people get an education. I also benefited from Lady Anita's generosity as she gave me a notebook.

Many adults today remember Mrs. Verdier for her kindness to the people of Nevis. Mrs. Verdier died many years ago. Her husband, Bud, kept the house.

He was an avid golfer and played mainly on the small golf course in Jones Estate near Cliff Dwellers.

After he also passed away, his daughter, Leslie Armentrout, inherited it and still owns it. Just like her mother, Leslie has given very much help to the people of Nevis.

Leslie came to Nevis back in the sixties after her parents built the house in Jones Estate. She got involved with the Pink Lily Breast Cancer Campaign. The Campaign raises funds to assist Nevisian women in getting annual mammograms. Leslie also has been active in tutoring school children so they can benefit fully from their education. Leslie has also regularly helped out as a volunteer for the annual Triathlon.

Marvin and Lou Anderson from Minnesota came to Nevis in the early sixties. Marve, as we called him, and Lou were also some of the greatest people you will find on this Earth. He bought an estate we call Mountain Paradise. He built a home at the top of Jessups, a little over a mile from the Island Road.

Jessups Road in those days was in very bad shape. There were lots of pot holes. Marve and his family would have to drive down that road to go to Charlestown to shop or to go to the beach. Marve was fond of water sports and especially fishing. So, with nobody doing anything about Jessups Road, Marve hired a contractor to fix the road from the bottom of the village at the intersection of the Island Main Road to the top at Mountain Paradise which is what he called his property. Then every few years Marve would spend thousands of dollars of his own money to maintain the road, not just for himself but for the general public.

Mr. Anderson also built a dam to collect rain water to help the people of Barnes Ghaut Village and Jessups. The water supply on Nevis at that time was not plentiful. Sometimes, when the weather was dry, you wouldn't get water in the Government pipelines for a long time, so people were hurting badly. Marve not only built a dam, but he also ran a pipeline so that the people of those two villages didn't have to travel too far to get water.

After Mr. Anderson left Nevis, the road he had built never got fixed again until 2007 when Premier Parry reconstructed the road from the bottom of Jessups to Barnes Ghaut and down to Cotton Ground Village. We, the people of St. Thomas Parish are very thankful for a man in the person of the late, great Marvin Anderson. He was truly a great American hero. He gave so much. May God give him eternal rest.

Marve also owned a butcher shop. They weekly butchered a young cow to make ground beef.

It was the first abattoir on St. Kitts or Nevis. They made ground beef and cut T-bone steaks to sell to the small hotels on Nevis. They also sold some to the grocery stores on Main Street in Charlestown who were their best customers on Nevis. The bones they used to sell for EC5 cents per pound. The people used to buy the beef bones to make soup. It was quite a treat for a giveaway price in those days on Nevis.

The Anderson family employed twenty persons on their farm. They also hired a manager named Santos Bowren, who died some seven years ago. Mr. Bowren was born in my village, Cotton Ground. He was General Manager of Mr. Anderson's estate since in the summer months the Andersons would go home to the US.

Every year the family would send down a huge wooden box of clothing--about ten pounds--to give to people who were in need. So people would go up to the Anderson house and get their clothes. This was a yearly event for more than twenty-five years.

Every Easter the Andersons would get in their Mini Moke and go around Nevis to give out sweets and chocolate for the children. They also contributed to many charities on Nevis.

Mr. Anderson was a very hard worker, but as he got along in age, he was no longer able to do what he had done in the past. So Marve decided to sell out and move back home. He lost his daughter in a snowmobile accident. This tragedy was devastating for the family.

Marve hung on for a couple of years, but then he died having reached his late seventies.

The people of Nevis lost a true friend and brother of Nevis. The Andersons truly played a great role on this little island creating jobs for our people. The Andersons were people everyone would like. They came to Nevis and did a great job helping our people. May Marve and "Mama Lou", as she was known to Nevisians, rest in peace.

There is an estate named Hermitage which goes back over three hundred years. It has been established that the Estate has one of the oldest wooden houses in the Caribbean. It still exists in very good condition and is currently used as a bar, dining room, living room, reading and games room and a bath. It is now run as a hotel thanks to Mr. Richard Lupinacci and his family who came to St. Kitts and Nevis more than three decades ago.

Richard was a manager for the Bank of America on St.Kitts. He came over to Nevis and loved the island. Richard and his family have put their all into making a difference for the people of Nevis. The Lupinaccis managed the Cliff Dwellers Hotel for a while in the eighties while I was working there. Later they managed the Zetlands Hotel until it was destroyed by Hurricane Hugo.

Subsequently, they have transformed the Hermitage Estate into a small hotel with the natural beauty of the locale and very attractive rooms.

The hotel is tucked away at the bottom of Nevis Peak surrounded by a beautiful rain forest. There are lots of green monkeys roving the Estate. They cause no harm to anyone. In fact, they will run away if approached.

The Lupinacci family has worked hard to keep the place beautiful. Since they arrived on Nevis, they have cared about our people.

They now employ a good number of Nevisians, several of whom have worked at the Hermitage for many years. Carrying on the long tradition of his family, Richard, Jr. now manages the hotel. Mr. Lupinacci treats his workers like family members.

For anyone visiting Nevis, the Hermitage is a must see destination. The lovely country inn is picture perfect. The Hermitage also serves great food like the special suckling pig roasted with all the trimmings. It is an outstanding buffet.

The family bought a restaurant by the sea from the Tyson family. It was built by Desmond Tyson back in the early eighties. It was a lovely place with a great view. The staff whipped up some delicious West Indian dishes including goatwater, curried goat, conch chowder and fish stew along with other local specialties. Mr. Tyson named the restaurant Beachcomber. It was just about fifty feet from the property which was developed into the Four Seasons Resort.

Mr. Tyson passed away in October, 2001, and left the restaurant to his family.

They ran it for a few years and then sold it to the Lupinaccis who also ran it for a few years. Being right on the water it gets battered whenever there are heavy storms. Eventually the Lupinaccis sold the place to the Four Seasons which put in a man-made reef to protect the property. Four Seasons now operates the restaurant as Mango.

The Lupinaccis are an outstanding family who have contributed much to Nevis in terms of charity and of helping the less privileged. We thank the family for caring about Nevis and its people and for many years of dedication to the island, a job very well done. May they continue to work for Nevis for many years to come.

The inn we call Golden Rock was not always a hotel. It was once a sugar plantation. The estate was owned by a man named Edward Huggins. He started to build in 1801. Mr. Huggins was a British doctor. In those days, Nevis was a colony of the United Kingdom. Mr. Huggins came to Nevis and developed a sugar plantation. He and his family ran the estate for many years.

As sugar became less profitable, many of the sugar estate owners left the island in search of a brighter future. Some traveled to England, some to the United States in search of the good life. And some went to more prosperous islands such as Barbados which was called the "Little Britain of the Caribbean".

In late 2010, I transported some folks from Barbados in my taxi.

These people could trace their family back four generations. Those who came to Nevis were part of the Maynard family, a family which owned many businesses in those days. In spite of their hard work, times were tough so they ended up selling out and leaving the island. If no buyer for the estate could be found, people would just abandon the land. Then the Crown would take it over and use the land to raise either sugar cane or cotton.

Slavery ended in 1834, the first Monday in August, but on St. Kitts and Nevis a black person was not truly free until 1838 because the plantation owners bargained with the Crown. They got an agreement that the former slaves had to work forty hours per week for their former slave owners. After the forty hours they were free to work for whomever they wished for pay, little as it was. From the plantation owners all they got for the forty hours of labor was a small food ration.

Life was hard for our ancestors, but after 1838, total freedom was declared. Some of the former slaves were able to own land. A few were successful, but most just worked for a pittance.

The Edward Huggins family moved from Nevis to the US. Many years later, one of Edward's descendents came back to Nevis and bought back part of the Golden Rock Estate. The family fell in love with Nevis and began to transform the property while maintaining its natural beauty. The property has one of the best views on Nevis.

The family turned the estate into a small hotel and started a tradition of serving the best lobster sandwiches you will find anywhere.

For more than forty years, the manager was Pam Barry, the daughter of the Mr. Huggins who transformed the estate from a sugar plantation to a plantation inn. She did a great job running Golden Rock, the home of her ancestors. Under her watchful eye, the landscaping was among the best in the Caribbean.

Mrs. Barry and her family love the people of Nevis and have employed and helped out many Nevisians. They continue working for the well-being of the people of Nevis, and we thank the family for choosing Nevis.

We owe special thanks to Mrs. Barry for her hands-on approach to make the Golden Rock Hotel such a wonderful place to visit and to dine. Golden Rock Hotel is on the East side of Nevis looking westward towards Mt. Nevis. When the weather is clear, there is a beautiful view of Montserrat, Antigua and the rock of Redonda which is just a few miles from Montserrat. It is totally picture perfect. Golden Rock gets a lot of rain, so I call this part of the island "monkey country". Many tourists stay in that part of the island making it a truly great place. Golden Rock has a very friendly staff eager to serve your every need.

The story of Nisbet Plantation begins with Frances Herbert Nisbet whose uncle was the President of the Nevis Assembly. In those days he was well-respected. Also at that time, he owned Montpelier Plantation, a sugar estate .

His niece, young Frances, got married at a very young age to an older man. When she was twenty-two years old, she was already a widow as she had lost her husband.

She met Admiral Horatio Nelson in 1787. They got married not long after. The wedding was at Fig Tree in a garden underneath a kapok tree. The tree is still very healthy after two hundred twenty-five years. The wedding party was at Montpelier Plantation, now a hotel. And party they did!

After many years passed, a young lady named Mary Pomeroy came from Malta and bought Nisbet Plantation and started building guest rooms. The Great House has remained intact until these days. Mary, as everyone on Nevis knew her, arrived here in 1950. In her late fifties she was very adventurous and a good airplane pilot. She came here when the Newcastle runway had only a gravel surface. She had flown in two World Wars and had been honored as a hero.

Mary came from a very prominent family. Her father was a Knight of Malta but Mary left all that good life to settle on Nevis. When there was no light in that part of the island, she brought a generator down to provide power for her hotel. She mostly ran it at night with the help of her employees, William Jeffers and Bertram Hanley. They did a good job. Mrs. Pomeroy stayed in Nevis until the early seventies. She sold Nisbet Plantation to the Boon family from our sister island, St. Kitts.

Mary moved to St. Martin and built a hotel on the beach which she called the Mary Boon.

Maybe she liked the surname of the family to whom she sold Nisbet Plantation and therefore chose that name for her new hotel. After many years, Mary decided to move to the US Virgin Islands. She settled on St. Croix, one of my favorite islands. She bought the Pink Fancy Hotel which she operated for many years, in fact, until she died in the 1990's.

Mary left St. Croix and was supposed to return from St. Maarten. Her plane went down. That was quite a disaster. The US Coast Guard sent many boats and planes searching for her, but they have never found Mary nor her plane.

Until this day the Pink Fancy Hotel is still operating under new management. Mary was 77 when she died, and she still had her pilot's license. Her father was still alive when Mary died. Her father, the Knight of Malta, was 102 years old and still going strong. Many guests that go to her hotel say that Mary never left. Her ghost still roams the hotel. She is still working but in a different role.

Mr. Boon did a great job improving the hotel at Nisbet Plantation. He planted lots of fruit trees and a lot of coconut palms. He also had his own private plane. Some times he would pick up guests in Antigua or on St. Maarten. He and his family had Nisbet Plantation humming about thirty years ago.

One day Jeff Boon took off from the Newcastle Airport. The plane quickly crashed and Mr. Boon lost his life.

It was a very sad day in Nevis. He was then just in his middle age. He had run that hotel very well.

His family sold the hotel shortly after his passing, and some Nevisians bought some of the shares. The biggest investor was a gentleman named George Barnum whose grandfather had the circus. Mr. Barnum and his wife, Elizabeth, were a very nice family. The added more rooms to the hotel and also built a villa for themselves close to the hotel. They operated the hotel for many years.

As George and Liz were getting on in years, they got together with the rest of the shareholders and in 1989, sold Nisbet Plantation to a Mr. David Dodwell who also operated a hotel in Bermuda. George died not long after he moved back to the States. The following year Liz passed away.

That couple did a lot of charity work for the hospital and infirmary, another American family who made a difference on Nevis.

Dodwell also did a lot to improve Nisbet Plantation. He retrained the staff so that in 2010, Nisbet was rated the best plantation inn in the Caribbean.

For more than fifty years, Nisbet Plantation has been evolving from good to the best. Being number one is quite an achievement. Most of the guests, as in most of the hotels on Nevis, are Americans.

Nisbet Plantation has many repeat guests. It is truly a paradise on the beautiful Atlantic Ocean. It's great for a visit to Nevis--a must see. Nisbet Plantation is a great place with its Great House which is almost three hundred years old. The first floor houses the kitchen, and the dining room is on the second floor. The grounds of Nevis Plantation are well maintained. The service is second to none.

There are lots more hotels in the Caribbean with good service, but Nisbet Plantation outshines them all. After more than fifty years of service, it is the longest-run hotel on Nevis.

The island of Nevis and the US have a very long relationship going back to 1607 when some English sailors came here and then sailed on to Virginia to start the first settlement on what was to become the US. For over four hundred years the people of Nevis and the US have been trading partners.

St. Kitts and Nevis is a country where travelers can visit and feel very much at home because of the warm love of its people. We treat our visitors with humility, love and respect no matter where they come from.

Nevis was one of the first islands that started the hotel trade back in 1778. The historic Bath Hotel was built by an Englishman with the free labor , of course, by the slaves. It is a job well done that has stood more than two hundred years.

The Bath Hotel was built so that guests, mostly from Europe, could take hot baths from natural hot springs to revive the body. The bath is still in use today.

Nowadays, most of our visitors come from the US. A few others come from Canada. Most of the development both on St. Kitts and Nevis is done by North Americans including Canadians. The US is our nation's most important trading and business partner. The US is still doing positive things in our world today. More than a thousand US citizens own property on Nevis and many are investing to give our people work--both short- and long-term employment.

We have many visitors to our shores who come by sea and by air to create employment for our citizens in our Federation. Our Government encourages more investment. It is a long-term goal. With many of our people employed , poverty will end. We, the people, have come a long way. Many of our young people are encouraged by our Government to own businesses and also to work for themselves.

Mr. & Mrs. Roger Staiger are now deceased. Both died in 2010 just three months apart. They had been married for more than sixty years. Dr. Staiger was a chemistry professor with a doctorate in the US . Everyone knew him.

Dr. Staiger came to Nevis fifty years ago with his wife who was also an educator. They built a home in the early sixties and after retiring, they moved to Nevis to enjoy their golden years.

Because of his love for golf, Roger decided to build his own golf course on his property, eventually developing 12 tees and greens on gently sloping land with great views of the Atlantic.

The Staigers were quite at home on Nevis. Because of the size of the property, including the golf course, they hired a few gardeners to keep up the maintenance of the golf course and surrounding gardens. Roger and Peggy were well loved on the island. They worked a lot with charity to help many of our young people. Since Dr. Staiger was a teacher all his life, he encouraged young Nevisians to go to school to get an education to be of benefit in their later years.

The Staigers were very pleasant people who loved Nevis and the Nevisians. Mrs. Staiger died on Nevis and is buried here. Roger died fewer than three months later. He just couldn't go on without the woman he loved for more than sixty years of marriage. What amazed me about that couple is their love for this island. They would do all in their power to help our people. We thank God for sending the Staigers to Nevis for fifty golden years on Paradise Island.

Mr. & Mrs. Roby came to Nevis in the early 1960's. They built themselves a home and named the place Hillcrest. Joe and Betty Roby came from the East coast of the US to retire and live out their golden years. They had bought a large parcel of land. and since Joe was fond of animals, he brought some sheep to raise on Nevis.

The sheep were of a special breed which produced very large animals. So many Nevisians at that time would take their ewes to be bred by Mr. Roby's ram in hopes of getting larger animals.

Joe Roby enjoyed raising animals. Betty Roby loved making clothes. Betty dressed very well for a middle-aged lady. Joe was not to be outdone. When they went out, they always were a well-dressed couple. Betty decided that she was tired of being at home, so she created her own line for sale. In 1965, she started making what we on Nevis call Carib Clothes. She made mostly men's shirts and women's dresses of 100% cotton fabric. The clothes would have embroidery around the front whether it was a shirt or a dress. We on Nevis call it "fancy work".

Mrs. Roby started with just three ladies in a room about twelve feet wide and sixteen feet long. Soon, more business started coming in and many people overseas started ordering clothes. My mother, Theodora Tyson, was Betty's top sewing lady. She was joined by Muriel Nisbett and Elvira Herbert. They made a good team. I remember my Mom would work late sometimes, and Mrs. Roby would always bring her home. Betty would also come to our house from time to time to give my mother extra work. My Mom had been making clothes at home since she was a teenager.

People loved Betty Roby's clothes. Both visitors and locals helped her business to keep growing.

After a few years, Mrs. Roby had to give up that location and move to another place closer to Main Street in Charlestown. Along with the bigger place she rented, she also had a much larger staff.

Some of the ladies made dresses and shirts. Some of them had to do embroidery work. Mrs. Roby would pay those doing fancy work by the amount they did in a day. The more they did, the more they would be paid.

It was a good business for all the ladies and for Betty, of course. And Nevis had its own brand name for many years! As time went on and Mrs. Roby reached her late seventies, she started getting ill and decided to take a back seat. So she hired a manager to run the business. In the early 1980's, Mr. & Mrs. Roby decided to retire, and they sold the company to a couple from Los Angeles.

We were sad on Nevis to see the Robys sell. The Robys started spending more time in the US for health reasons, but they kept their home on Nevis. Betty still stayed very much involved with charity work here on Nevis. The Robys loved Nevis, and the people of Nevis loved them as well.

Betty died in the early nineties leaving Joe alone. They had lost an older son in the Vietnam War, but they had one son still living. Joe continued to visit Nevis to spend the winters in his home here. In the Spring of 1993, after having been in ill health for a while, Joe Roby passed away.

Ripp and Coffie Todd who purchased Caribbee Clothes kept the name brand and expanded the business. Mrs. Todd managed the business and her husband handled the finances. After a few years, in the mid-eighties, Coffie took ill. She was taken to Alexandra Hospital where she died leaving Ripp Todd all alone. The church was packed at Coffie's funeral, attended by her friends and her large staff. She was buried on Nevis at the Bath Cemetery.

After Mrs. Todd passed away, her husband tried to keep up the business, but he didn't manage to do it. So after a few years, Mr. Todd gave up and moved back to the States where he later died.

Caribbee Clothes is no longer on Nevis, but those ladies did a great job and employed young people to make a difference. May their souls rest in peace. They gave their best for this island, and its people will keep them forever in our hearts.

The McFaddens arrived on Nevis in the mid-sixties and built a lovely home on the top of Ridge Road hill overlooking Oualie Beach. Mrs. McFadden was a school teacher in the United States. She came to Nevis every summer, and when she retired, she and her husband also came down in the winter. Sometimes her daughter and her son-in-law came and visited.

Mrs. McFadden had a great love for Nevis and its people. She was very much concerned about the young people of the Island. She wanted them to get a good education.

She would bring down books from the US to give to the children, including me and some of my school friends.

The McFaddens were looking forward to a happy retirement on Nevis, but it was a shock when her husband of many years took ill and passed away suddenly. Since Mrs. McFadden was left alone, she would come to Nevis with her daughter who took good care of her. Even though Mrs. McFadden was getting on in age, her love for Nevis and its children never diminished.

As she grew old and no longer able to travel, she gave the property to her daughter, Lynne Hubbard, and her husband, Gordon, who also love Nevis and so they spend much time here each year. Her daughter was also a teacher and shares her mother's role of helping the people of Nevis.

Jack and Jessie Williams from the State of Michigan came to Nevis and loved it so they bought a property on the rocks near Oualie Beach and built a home there. It was completed in 1968. Jack was still working for Ford Motors in Michigan so they could only come for short visits until he retired. After that, they came for longer stays every year for many years. The house they own was built on solid rock so they named it "ON THE ROCKS". It's a lovely property on the best beach site on Nevis. After many years, Jessie took ill at home in the US and passed away.

Jack returned to Nevis the year following his wife's death. His gardener, Nigel Browne, normally went to work daily to help with the lawn and the plantings.

After Jessie's death, following some forty years of marriage, Jack was devastated. One morning, Nigel came to work knowing that Jack normally woke up early. But that morning he never did. Nigel called to him thinking Jack was still asleep. There was no answer so Nigel went inside and discovered that Jack was dead. He had died in his sleep. Jack was lonely and apparently lost the will to live after Jessie died.

They were a great American family as is their daughter who was raised on Nevis and who now loves the Island as much as her parents did. The Williams were truly a great couple who loved Nevis and gave to many causes focussed on the needs of the Nevisian people.

Another couple, Sykes and Florence Manning, was a complete pair or so I would call them. She was his Queen and Sykes was King. They visited Nevis for many years before they decided to build a home here. They built a house in the Cliff Dwellers area in Jones Estate. All of Nevis loved them. When there was a dance on Nevis, Sykes and Florence had the floor. The young people could not keep up with them. Sykes loved gardening. He had a large garden with which he had some local help of course. This was an American family who totally devoted themselves to Nevis and its people.

After many years on Nevis, Sykes died and was buried on Nevis. Florence lived on for many years after. Her daughter dedicated herself to taking care of Florence until she also died. The daughter is now retired. She and her husband now live full time on Nevis and continue the good work her parents started back in the sixties.

There was an American woman who came from the East Coast of the US in the mid-sixties and started a gift shop in downtown Charlestown not very far from Alexander Hamilton's birthplace. Her name was Arlene Swift. Miss Swift also did crafts locally and also hired a craftsman who would weave baskets made out of mountain lumber. They would weave coconut fronds and make placemats and hand fans. It was a good business. Their shop was a place you could go to and get handcrafted goods.

Miss Swift would also go to Newcastle village famous for making clay pottery including coal pots, ash trays, flower pots and candle holders. Miss Swift would take them to her place of business. Many of our early visitors would buy her crafts and take them back to their home country.

Miss Swift stayed on Nevis for many years. She left in the early eighties and sold her business to another American lady. Arlene Swift moved back to the US. She was of advanced age and decided it was time to retire and be close to her family since she was single with no children.

Since Arlene left Nevis, many more people have gotten involved with handicraft work and in making clay flower pots, coal pots, and many other sorts of handicrafts. The Nevis Island Administration built a Craft House and has classes for young people to learn the various crafts, skills which they can then pass on to future generations. Consequently, one can find lots of art work on Nevis.

The Parmenter Building was owned by Miss Bernadine Parmenter whose father's name was Harold Parmenter, of Jewish descent. It was one of the largest building blocks in Charlestown. Harold started his business early in the 1900's and worked for many years. He also owned the Belmont Estate on Nevis. He did a great business selling dry goods and liquor in his store. Harold had several children. One of his sons moved to the US at an early age to do his own thing and seek a better education. He didn't have any interest in the family business. He did very well in the US. Harold and his wife and their other two children ran the business on Nevis for many years. Harold and his wife passed away back in the early fifties.

Miss Bernadine Parmenter continued with the business in Charlestown. That way she was the one and only Queen then in town. She never got married. After she advanced in age, she leased most of the downstairs to a young businessman named Tony Horner.

Tony Horner was born on Montserrat, the son of a British family. He came to Nevis many years ago and started a business on Main Street in Charlestown. He opened the very first self-service supermarket in Charlestown. He also brought in one of the first electric ice cream makers. He did a great business.

He also opened the Rookery Nook. It was the place to be, especially for Americans. When their wives went shopping, the old boys would gather there until the girls came back and joined them. Tony Horner ran the Nook for many years. It was a great place in Charlestown, and the American visitors loved it.

The Nook had a large courtyard and lovely flamboyant trees that bloomed all summer long. It was very pretty. The front of the business faced Main Street and the back looked out toward the sea in the direction of St. Kitts. That place is no longer in business.

The Hunkins family bought the property and transformed it. They rebuilt the whole block in a Caribbean style architecture. It now houses the Bank of Nova Scotia and Lime, our principal telephone company. There are also a few stores and some off-shore investment companies.

Tony was not just a store owner. He was also a car dealer. Tony never did marry, but he was a ladies man. After many years of business on Nevis, Tony retired. He passed away at age 71, a life well spent.

There was a couple from the US named Joe and Mrs. Bailey. They would come to Nevis in November each year and leave in April. They were retired and spent time on Nevis for many years.

They also gave a lot to charity on Nevis. They loved Nevis. It was their second home. Mrs. Bailey passed away in the States and was buried there. Joe Bailey still came to Nevis for many years after his wife's death.

The Nook was his favorite place to hang out even when he was well advanced in age. When he left to return to the States every Spring, there was a sign at the bar saying, "Joe Bailey will return". That he did the next Fall.

When he was no longer able to move around as before, Joe sold his house to a young local family. Joe died in the US a few years ago.

I remember a man named Curtis Mathis who came to the Islands in the early seventies and set up a television factory on St. Kitts. It was the first of its kind in the Federation. The business did so well that a few years later Mr. Matthew opened a branch on Nevis making it possible for several Nevisians to get jobs making televisions. Lots of young people were employed by the factory.

The second largest employer after the Nevis Island Administration is the Four Seasons Resort which was built by a Canadian family. Mr. Sharp came to Nevis many years ago and loved the Island. He expanded his hotel chain on Nevis by building the Four Seasons Resort which employs over 700 people. The Resort, the largest hotel on the Island, plays a vital role on Nevis and helps to stimulate the local economy. Many people in addition to its employees benefit from its presence. Folks outside the hotel such as farmers and fishermen and many others don't work for the hotel but have income because of it.

Nevisian restaurants depend on the hotel to bring guests to their tables. The guests at Four Seasons often go to the Island Inns for a meal in a new setting which of course is a boon for their business. The Four Seasons is good for Nevis as everyone wins.

Many celebrities come to Nevis because of the Four Seasons.

For example, Oprah Winfrey, former US President, George H. Bush, Harry Belafonte, Chris Evert Lloyd, Kelly Ripa, John Travolta, Britney Spears, Robert Plante, Mary Travers and many more have vacationed here.

Mrs. Benjamin and her late husband built a Great House at Cliff Dwellers in Jones Estate. It was truly a great house. In those days it was one of the largest in that area. As time went by, much larger houses were built in that same area.

Mrs. Benjamin's husband was ailing. He died a few years after the house was completed, but Mrs. Benjamin kept coming to Nevis every winter and stayed here until the Spring. Being all alone with no husband, and getting on in age, she sold her house to a couple named John and Rosemary Gullet.

John was a very good lawyer who spent much of his time in the US. Rosemary spent most of the winter on Nevis so in her spare time, she would do charity work such as volunteering for the Red Cross. She would make sure that young people not only went to school but also that they had the necessary materials to work profitably in school.

Rosemary was one of the pillars of the Fun Fair along with Margaret Lyman. All the money that those ladies raised went to charity. Some of the funds were distributed to the poor and other funds were granted to the infirmary at the hospital.

Rosemary worked for many years helping the poor on the Island of Nevis because of her love for the people. She always said that being able to help others made life worthwhile. She was a true Christian. Rosemary took ill in late 1980. She returned to the US for medical treatment but she died. May she rest in peace.

Rosemary Gullet was a great lady. She was an American who came to Nevis when it was very quiet. She made a difference in the lives of many of our young people and so many of our senior citizens as well. Miss Rosemary—that is what everyone called her—came from Washington, DC, to Nevis looking for property.

I must mention Donald and Paula Flemming who first came to Nevis in 1987. They found the Island to be very pretty and the people warm and friendly. Because of their love of Nevis, the Island is now their second home. They do a lot of charity work on Nevis and spend most of the winter here helping the young people on the Queen of the Caribbees.

Both Paula and Donald, who had long careers as educators at all levels, have consulted with teachers in the Nevis schools, helping them to understand modern techniques of instruction. They have provided reading books to students who had none at home. They have tutored students one-on-one helping them to advance in their studies.

For years, they coordinated the volunteers for the annual Nevis Triathlon, an event which has brought many visitors from overseas to our shores as well as international attention to Nevis.

The Newcastle Police Station has a tradition of hosting a neighborhood party to get to know the folks in the village as well as seasonal visitors to the Island. Paula and Don have regularly made contributions to support the party. They also attend the function and bring their friends along so that they can interact with the local community.

And like many of our friends from abroad, they employ Nevisians on a year-round basis, as well as many local service people, to maintain their property here. They have actively helped the Nevis Historical and Conservation Society on many occasions.

And they have regularly adopted dogs to help with the work of the Animal Rescue and Caring organization. Furthermore, they are active in roadside and beach litter clean-up. And, as I mentioned in the Acknowledgements, without the Flemmings it would have been very difficult for me to get my books published.

David Robinson came to Nevis from the United States and along with his late wife, Joan, worked hard to preserve the history of Nevis. The Robinsons were active in promoting the mission of the Nevis Historical and Conservation Society. Joan was active in organizing beach clean-ups and the monitoring of beach erosion. This couple was truly dedicated to Nevis and its people and the Island owes them a deep debt of gratitude.

I met Amba Trott many years ago. Amba is a man of many talents who always encourages our young people to get a good education and to preserve Nevis' history for generations to come. Amba's mother was born on Nevis—his father was from New York City—but his parents moved to Canada in search of a better life.

So Amba and his siblings were born in Canada, but his parents never forgot about Nevis. They moved back to the Island after they retired and spent many years here. Their children also came to Nevis and have contributed much to our society.

Amba is a great playwright, but he has written many other types of pieces. My favorite is his best-selling book, "Nonsense in Nevis", a collection of satirical anecdotes and essays. People like Amba Trott make our Island a better place by bringing such talent here. We are grateful for his many contributions.

Mrs. Lillian O'Brien was a lady who dedicated her life to serve God and Country. We here on Nevis called her "Mom" because she had so much love not only for her own eleven children, but for everyone she met. She was also a great hostess and gave lots of parties.

Mrs. O'Brien was born on Nevis in 1887 in the village of Barnes Ghaut. Her mother was a farmer. Her father, a white American, came from the US in the late 1870's and bought the Tower Hill Estate to raise cattle and grow potatoes as well as many other crops. His name was John Morrisey.

After many years on Nevis, he sold the Tower Hill Estate and returned to the US. He was then in his late sixties. I understand that he kept writing to "Mom" for some time.

"Mom" had two children on Nevis, Edmund and Oscar Morrisey. Her father decided to send for her, so she left her two boys with her mother and went to New York where she got a job as a live-in with an American couple. On weekends she would go to help her father who was getting on in age. Some time later she sent for her sons. Since "Mom's" father was born in the US, it was easy to gain entry for her sons.

Lillian got married in New York. Her father was her best man. Her husband, Mr. Daniel, was from St. Thomas. He was doing business in New York and on St. Thomas where he had five rental properties. The couple ended up having nine children which, added to Lillian's two sons from Nevis, made eleven. Edmund and Oscar joined the US military and traveled all over the world. Both took part in World War II and Korea having served their adopted country for many years.

Mrs. O'Brien's husband passed away some years later leaving her to care for his nine children. A few years later, Lillian married a Mr. Browne who was much older than she. He also passed away. She then married twice more but both of these marriages ended in the death of the husband.

Lillian had a neighbor, Francis O'Brien, whose wife, an older New Yorker, had also passed away. All of Lillian's eleven children had grown up and left the home.

So she was feeling lonely and Francis was too, so they got married late in 1950.

Lillian brought her new husband to her home country, Nevis. Francis loved the Island, so he bought several acres of land in the village of Cotton Ground. Shortly thereafter, they started building a home. We called Francis "Pops" to match our name for Lillian, "Moms". After the house was finished, the O'Briens decided to build a shop.

They employed a young lady to run the business. Since Lillian was a good cook, she prepared a lot of dishes to sell in the shop. Business was booming in that corner store! As a kid, my mother would send me to wash their dishes. Since Moms was such a good cook, I enjoyed doing dishes for her because at the end of my work, I would get a treat.

After a few years of running the corner store, the O'Briens decided to quit for they were getting on in years. So they rented out the corner store to a Mr. Hill, a young family man. Well, in 1974, Moms had a stroke so she couldn't do as much as she previously loved to do. Her children would come down from the US to visit her and help her out since her health didn't seem to be improving.

Moms passed away in October of 1975 at the age of 87 years leaving her husband, Francis, her eleven children and more than twenty grandchildren behind.

Francis lived on for another fifteen years, passing away in 1990 at ninety-two. Both Lillian and Francis were buried at St. Thomas Church in Cotton Ground.

Roslyn Woodburn was born in the US; her husband was born on St. Kitts. Mrs. Woodburn first visited St. Kitts and Nevis in 1960 with their two young daughters. They were invited to visit Nevis because Mr. Woodburn's classmate, Mr. Claxton, was in the Real Estate business here. He had an office on Shaw's Road in Newcastle.

The Woodburns bought a few acres and two years later, since they were close to retirement age, they started building a vacation home to get away from the cold winters. But Mr. Woodburn took ill and returned to the States for treatment.

The girls and their mother stayed on for a while, but Roslyn became very concerned about her husband's health. So she took her children to the US to see their Daddy.

Mr. Woodburn passed away in 1963, but Roslyn kept the property on Nevis and moved here full time after she retired. She became involved with the Red Cross and donated lots of time and materials to help the needy. Roslyn attended the Anglican Church and was quite active with the Mothers Union of St. James Parish.

Roslyn hosted lots of parties for her friends and neighbors but her true calling was caring for our people and working to preserve the history of the Island. Mrs. Woodburn died in August of 1985.

One of her daughters still owns the property that Roslyn and her husband bought back in 1960.

Another great American was the late Mr. Abraham who came to Nevis from the East Coast in the early 1960's. Along with his wife, he worked hard on all the charity efforts here on the Island. Though his wife passed away many years before him, he kept coming back to Nevis for many years.

Even in his nineties he didn't give up his efforts to preserve the history of Nevis. He believed that young people must understand the story of their past. They must learn how hard our forefathers and mothers had to work to create a better future for the children's children.

Back in the sixties, Mr. Donavan, an American from the East Coast of the US, came to Nevis on his yacht which was shipwrecked at Jones Bay. He had to spend quite a bit of time on Nevis before he could leave since he had to wait for his yacht, a large wooden forty footer, to be repaired.

Mr. Donavan was quite a fellow. While he was on Nevis, he sought work and since he was a good carpenter, he got a job with the Cliff Dwellers Construction Company. Whenever he had a spare moment he would work on his yacht. A year went by and several months more as he caulked his boat, sealed it with tar and gave it a fresh coat of paint. When he had finished, the boat was beautiful. It was master craftmanship—a well done job.

Some time later, Donavan got a group of men to help him push the yacht back into the sea. But he kept working at his job at Cliff Dwellers.

One morning, everyone was looking for him. Donavan and his boat had disappeared. He said no goodbyes and he had no farewell party. It was a mystery. He probably is dead by now because all this happened back in the sixties. He was a fellow about 60 years of age. No one ever heard a word about the "mystery man" after his disappearance.

John & Allie Guilbert came to Nevis from the US. John started a horseback riding business which he ran for many years. He took the tourists up the trail and on the beach. Local students got a discount. Anyone who didn't know how to ride could be taught how to do so. John also did lots of charity work for the people on Nevis. He and his wife, Allie, gave many hours of volunteer labor working to keep Nevisian history alive.

Allie also worked as a popular disc jockey and announcer on a local radio station. She also hosted a great talk show. I loved to listen to the way she educated our young people on Nevis and elsewhere.

John also worked for many years for the Nevis Historical and Conservation Society at the Alexander Hamilton House to keep the history of Nevis available for future generations.

In 1957, a Mr. Moore came from Wisconsin to Nevis prospecting.

He learned that the Tower Hill Estate was up for sale so he went on a tour of the property. He loved what he saw, so he bought the property with the intention of giving it to his daughter, Rose, and her new husband, George West.

Rose and George came down from the States to run the property. They had lots of cows. When the herd got too big, from time to time, they would sell off a few. They also worked a lot of land.

They had a manager who had worked for the Estate before the Wests owned it. In fact, he spent most of his life working there. His name was William Nisbett, but everyone called him "Pappy". When Rose and George were off Island, Pappy would run the Estate. He would ride his horse to town to get money to pay the boys who worked on the Estate. Using his own money he would bring home groceries on his horse to cook for his staff. Pappy managed the farm well.

It was large by Nevis' standards, some 960 acres. He andthe boys who worked on the Estate raised seven acres of sweet potatoes as well as lots of bananas and fresh vegetables. In those days, there were not so many monkeys. Some of the older folks used to eat monkey meat but nowadays few people eat it.

Pappy worked for the Wests until he was eighty two and couldn't ride his horse anymore. He bought a donkey which was easier for him to mount. Pappy died at age 85 in June of 1976.

Rose appointed the second in command, a Mr. Martin, as General Manager to look after the property when she and her husband were back in the States. As time went on, the Wests moved back to the States permanently and left Mr. Martin to run the Estate. Martin was a Christian, and, like old Nisbett before him, he was trustworthy.

Mr. Moore still came to Nevis occasionally. His wife had passed away, so Mr. Moore came with his son, Bruce, until he was very old and no longer able to travel. He died some twenty-five years ago.

George and Rose planned to spend a lot of time on Nevis so they shipped down a camping trailer (called caravans locally) to live in. In those days, only a few people on Nevis had electrical power if they lived off the main Island road.

After living in the caravan for some time, Rose built a house on some property she owned on the beach. She put in a large cistern knowing that water was not plentiful on the Island. Rose had to pay for lots of posts (telephone poles) to get electric current to her beach house in the mid-sixties.

Rose had a lot of horses. She and George would ride to town on horseback to get materials for the Estate. The Wests also had a tractor. Rose was able to handle that tractor very well. When I was little, she would come down to Cotton Ground on her tractor and all the villagers would be amazed to see a lady at the controls. She was a very skilled woman.

Rose's parents, the Moores, would come to visit their daughter when it was possible. Mr. Moore had a ranch back in the US with a large herd of cattle.

Rose turned over the running of the Estate to her brother, Bruce. Mr. Martin also passed away in his mid-eighties. Most of the other Tower Hill staff has now retired and some have passed away.

The lower part of Tower Hill was sold by Bruce Moore to local developer, Deon Daniel who has called his project "Fern Hill".

Mike Foster started flying to Nevis over thirty years ago. In the old days, Mike flew to Nevis for Balkie Airlines for a few years. It was hard to get to Nevis for our North American friends, so Balkie Airlines did a lot of good for our early tourism trade with the US and Canada. When Balkie Airlines pulled out of Nevis, there was no direct flight here making it very difficult to get here.

Mike Foster, who was no stranger to Nevis, decided to take up the mantle and form his own airline which he called Coastal Air. Mike has made direct flights to Nevis from St. Croix for more than 25 years on his own airline. Mike's contribution has done a lot for Nevis making it easy to travel from St. Croix to Nevis and back. Mike saw the need and he filled the gap.

Mike not only brings passengers to our Island, he also brings lots of cargo here. Nevisians who have family on St. Croix often send food and medical supplies with Mike for their relatives. Mike also delivers packages for our ex-pats.

Coastal Air flies to Nevis three times per week: Sundays, Wednesdays, and Fridays and at other times by special arrangement.

My first book, "Ozzie's Odyssey", was brought to me by Mike so that I could distribute it to interested readers. It would have been difficult for me to get the books shipped to Nevis if it weren't for Mike. I should also mention that Mike also gives back to Nevis. Every year for the past many years Mike has sponsored a young Nevisian lady for Culturama. Some of the women he has helped have become Queen of Culturama.

The Meguids came to Nevis in 1980, and, like so many other visitors, they fell in love with the Island and its people. Adelaide and Sally were looking for a place to invest. They looked at many tracts of land, but were most taken by Round Hill Estate. There is a great view of Round Hill to the West, the sea and St. Kitts to the North and Mt. Nevis to the Southeast.

 They purchased many acres near the top of Shaw's Road, and began building a series of condos, the first on Nevis. They completed the first units as well as the pool and restaurant, in 1989. The business, which is now a hotel, has one of the best views on Nevis, beautiful landscaping and luxury apartments second to none.

After all these years, Dr. Meguid still keeps the property in tip-top condition. He employs a great staff who welcome you and make you feel like royalty by the service the hotel offers. The food in the restaurant is great and is served with a smile.

Many of the guests are repeaters. The hotel also has a Conference Center to accommodate large groups. Its romantic setting is also great for picture perfect weddings, and many have been held there over the years.

The Meguids also operate a restaurant on the beach near the airport called Pizza Beach. In addition to pizza, the restaurant also serves a variety of local dishes.
It it is a popular place with Nevisian families who also enjoy the take-out service.

Joe and Martha Murphy came to Nevis from the US back in the early nineties and stayed at the Four Seasons Resort. They then bought a villa on the Four Seasons golf course. Soon, the Murphys decided to invest in Nevis to create work for Nevisians. In Charlestown, they bought land and developed a fun park called Caribbean Cove. Local families would take their children there on weekends to enjoy the rides and the good food.

The Murphys also bought some property on Fig Tree Road and started clearing land where they built the only botanical garden on Nevis. It has trees and plants from all over the world—truly a visitors' paradise. In addition to the lovely gardens, including an indoor tropical collection and a rose garden with interesting statuary, there is also a restaurant and a gift shop which offers both local and imported exotic gifts.

Nevisians and local students can visit the gardens at a reduced price.

The business is currently owned by Christie Douglas who owns a similar property on Anguilla. Ms. Douglas has demonstrated a desire to contribute to the betterment of Nevis.

Dan Macmullin moved to Nevis from Canada with his family years ago. After running a business here for several years, he became increasingly concerned that a lot of young Nevisians, especially, boys and young men, were getting involved in gang activities. They began imitating the urban hoodlums of North American cities which the locals unfortunately learned about with the advent of cable television.

Dan started a youth group to direct young men away from gang violence. He started an antigang campaign to teach young men that there is more to life than getting in trouble and ending up in jail.

He brought an expert on gang behaviors to Nevis from Canada. This individual had done a lot of work in Canadian cities so he was well experienced in dealing with young people. He conducted a number of workshops and met with the leaders of the local government to offer advice.

Dan also visits the prisons on St. Kitts and Nevis and works with the inmates to encourage them to make something of themselves once they are out of prison. He is working hard to help all Nevisians be better citizens of their community.

In Cotton Ground Village Dan got together with some of our young people and repaired the old Police Station in Cotton Ground. It is now a Youth Center where young people can listen to and learn how to play music and other skills. Even some of the prisoners get involved in learning new skills so that when they leave prison, they can be successful.

Marty Salvato was better known as the "Goat Lady" because of her love for that animal. She would nurse sick and injured goats back to health, and so many who discovered a troubled animal would bring it to Marty for repair and recovery. She had a big buck named Big Boy who was truly a specimen of maleness. He liked all the ladies, both goats and the human kind and never failed to show his appreciation.

Sadly, for Nevis, Marty and her husband, Danny Burns, moved to Grenada a few years ago leaving a gap in our animal care sector.

Don and Carol Peterson hailed from Texas. They came to Nevis to retire but due to their love of plants, they started a landscaping business called "Absolutely Bushed". They had a nursery on their Fig Tree property where they grew the plants to be sold. They hired several Nevisians to help them operate the business. In Charlestown, all the banks would rent indoor plants from the Petersons.

They did a lot of work all over Nevis. They put in a lot of our royal palms and Christmas palms. Don grew most of the plants he sold in his own nursery in the back yard.

Don was a very tall fellow, about 6'6". After being on Nevis for many years, and working hard, not only landscaping, but charity work as well, Don and Carol sold the business and returned to the US where Don died a few years ago.

Vince Hubbard, historian and writer, came to Nevis more than twenty years ago and started Morning Star Holding Co. That Company was one of the earliest off-shore banking companies on Nevis, an industry which pays a lot of taxes to the Nevis Island Administration.

I knew Mr. Hubbard well. He loved history, a field he studied and researched for many years. He loved to write about the islands of the Caribbean. His best-selling book, "Swords, Ships and Sugar", tops the list in Nevis and St. Kitts.

Vince was from the US, but he spent most of his later life on Nevis. He worked hard to preserve the Island's history. He located sunken cannons and warships and helped to identify their origins. He led tours to historic sites and lectured on the background. And he filled every conversation with anecdotes about historical matters.

Sadly, in 2012, Vince took a bad fall from his balcony— the railing had been removed due to construction—and he was severely injured. He was forced to return to the US for treatment and care, and after several months of struggle with the effects of his injuries, he passed away. His legacy on Nevis will be long remembered.

Barbara (Bobbie) and Edward (Wally) Wilson came to Nevis from Pennsylvania in the late 1970's. They bought land in Jones Estate and built a home there with a million dollar view. It is paradise on Earth surrounded by Round Hill on the East, Mt.Nevis on the West and the Caribbean Sea and St. Kitts to the North. Barbara's love for gardens and plants led to the creation of a landscape which is breathtaking.

So every year, Barbara and Edwad spent most of the winter on Nevis. Since their home is close to Round Hill, the monkeys come to visit daily much to Bobbie's chagrin. The Wilsons were great entertainers and invited their expat friends and neighbors to join them for refreshments and conversation.

After some years, Edward took ill, but he would still come to Nevis as much as he could until he was no longer able to travel. He died several years ago, but Mrs. Wilson still comes back to her home in Nevis every year.

Barbara's cousin, Gloria, came to Nevis with her husband, Frank Coulom, to visit Barbara and Edward on their retirement.

They liked what they saw and bought property and built a lovely winter home high up on Ridge Road. Now they spend most of the winter on Nevis and return to the US for the summer.

Dr. Chandy Jacob has made Nevis his home for many years. His dear wife, Elizabeth, is a tower of strength and support for her husband.

Dr. Jacob has been caring for our sick and elderly for more than twenty years. He also makes house calls for those people who can't travel to his office in Charlestown. Dr. Jacob always finds the time to care for the sick and the shut-ins. He goes the extra mile to make sure all his patients are cared for. You can call him 24/7; as long as he is on Island, he will come to assist you.

I wish we had more doctors like him—so dedicated to his work. He always puts people first at all times. In addition to his private practice, he is also the physician on call at the Four Seasons Resort and he serves the Nevis Island Administration as Coroner and Medical Examiner.

Kelly Ripa, co-hostess of the morning US talk show, "Live with Kelly and Michael", has visited Nevis several times including enthusiastically enjoyed stops at the world-famous Sunshine's Beach Bar on Pinney's Beach. As a result of her fondness for Nevis, Kelly has talked about the Island on her nationally televised program many times thus promoting tourism to Nevis.

Karen Peterson, a US citizen, came to Nevis from Africa where she met her husband, Nevisian John Yearwood, while doing Peace Corps service. Karen and John, along with John's brother, Alastair, started operating a restaurant on Oualie Beach which they later expanded into guest cottages and then a hotel.

Karen managed the business for a while, but then returned to teaching.

She taught Spanish and did administrative work at the Lyn Jeffers School in Charlestown for many years helping local young people to learn a second language, one spoken by many of our newcomers from the Dominican Republic.

Vicki Knorr and her younger son, Greg, came to Nevis from St. Croix. The Knorr family had moved from the US to St. Croix and had worked there for many years.

Vicki's husband passed away quite some time before she and Greg decided to come to our Island. Greg's older brother returned to the States.

Greg and Vicki visited the old Croney House which at the time was in delapidated condition. The property had been a sugar plantation and part of the old mill is still intact. The former Great House was a breeding house during slavery times.

They bought the property anyway and with the help of a team of Nevisians, they restored the property and created Old Manor Hotel near the South end of the Island in Gingerland. The Knorrs did a fine job to put the property in a beautiful condition.

After many years of successfully running the hotel and having employed many Nevisians in the process, Vicki and Greg decided to retire from the business in part because Vicki was getting on in years. They sold the property to an American lady who is currently in the process of cleaning up the place with hopes to sell.

Sybil Seigfried of Pennsylvania bought a property called Yam Seed which had been built many years before. It was on the waterfront near the airport with a view of St. Kitts and Booby Island. Sybil fixed up the main house and started a bed and breakfast business which was successful for many years. She employed local staff to assist her with the household tasks and upkeep of the grounds.

She added many plants to the gardens making it a beautiful area. She attracted guests from many places and being close to the airport, she accommodated the flight crews at times.

Sybil made a conscious effort to relate to the locals and her neighbors. As the years went by, Sybil started taking ill and had to spend more time back in the US. Eventually, she lost her battle with cancer and died back in the US.

Sheila Williams came to Nevis from Canada many years ago to visit her in-laws on the Island. I first met her in 1988 at her father-in-law's funeral. A few years later she returned to Nevis with Eddy, her spouse, and started a restaurant in Charlestown named Eddy's. It was the place to be. Wednesday night they had a happy hour attended by many locals and lots of ex-pats. The restaurant also had a great menu.

Later, Sheila and Eddy bought land at Cade's Bay Estate and started building The Inn at Cade's Bay. It is located on the beach with a great view of St. Kitts. The construction created several jobs for Nevisians.

Sheila built a new restaurant on the beach and called it Tequila Sheila's. It was a great success which she managed for many years.

After putting their all into the business, the family decided to sell the property in order to have more free time.

The Hoen family came to Nevis several years ago and bought a lovely property on the edge of Fern Hill Estate in an area developed by Deon Daniel many years ago. Because the property is high up, the views are great both of the mountains and the ocean.

Hudson always stopped to ask walkers if they wanted a ride. That way he came to be friends with many locals. He also hiked and rode bikes with local men and women. And Winston Crooke could always count on Hudson to help out with the Triathlon. Hudson's wife, Lynne, a former math teacher, helped many a school child to improve their math skills so they could keep up with their classmates.

Bonnie Berlinghof first came to Nevis over thirty years ago on vacation. She came from New York where she still maintains a residence. Winters are spent on Nevis now that she has retired. Bonnie bought a lovely home in Jones Estate from an American named Paul Peter. Bonnie's family has come down to visit from time to time including her parents and her brothers with their families. Her parents lived a long life. Her mother was over a hundred years of age when she passed away.

Bonnie's friend, Nikolai and his uncle, Misha, sometimes came to visit her. They had a lot of fun on Nevis during these visits including house parties to which they invited both visitors and locals. Nick was a great entertainer. He could sing well. Misha, early in the morning always said, "Life is beautiful! Ho! Ho! Ho! Life is beautiful!"

Misha, who was born in Russia, lived in Canada for many years. Both Nick and Misha have passed away, but Olga, Misha's daughter, still comes to stay at Bonnie's residence. Olga also lives in Canada but spends a few months on Nevis every year. When Bonnie is away, Olga takes care of her home in Nevis.

Bonnie was in the Peace Corps for several years. She volunteers for programs designed to help Nevisian children. She also gives a lot of time to the Animal Rescue and Kindness (ARK) which aims to care for stray animals on Nevis. And she contributes time and money to various charity efforts on the Island.

Walter and Elaine Schubert came to Nevis from the US in the sixties and because of their love for the people of the Island, they sponsored two Nevisian women for graduate study in the US. The women completed their professional degrees and returned to Nevis to contribute their skills to helping others on the Island as well as being role models for other young Nevisian women. Walter and Elaine also gave equipment to the Physical Therapy Department at Alexandra Hospital so that the staff there could better serve the Nevisian public.

Rosemary Sullivan, a writer and photographer from Quebec, has been coming to Nevis for many years. She has produced two books about Nevis and its people, both of which are loaded with her photographs of folks of all ages, genders and walks of life. She has made an effort to meet people and to hear their stories. In fact, she has played a key role in the development of the Oral History Project.

Rosemary gives slide shows to benefit the Nevis Historical Society and she gives her photos free of charge to any Nevisian who can find a picture of him or herself among Rosemary's extensive collection. Rosemary loves Nevis deeply and helps those in need in any way she can.

The Medical University of the Americas (MUA) was established on Nevis quite some time ago. The school has brought prosperity to the Island because many local folks have gone into the rental business to accommodate the housing needs of the students. Nevisians are continuing to build apartment complexes in the vicinity of the school which is located on the Eastern side of the Island near St. James Anglican Church. Local farmers also benefit as the students buy much of their produce. And of course all the Island restaurants and shops gain income because of the student expenditures.

The school employs several Nevisians in a variety of capacities and buys goods and services locally. A further benefit is that the school offers free tuition to any Nevisian student who can qualify for admission.

Cottle Church was built around 1824 by local plantation owner, Thomas Cottle. He owned Round Hill Estate where he grew sugar cane and raised animals. In the days of slavery, only whites could attend services at the Anglican Churches.

Thomas was a good man, I would say. He believed that his slaves should be able to worship God along side of him and his family. Since other whites did not agree, he built his own church where he alone had the say. And until his death, he and his slaves worshipped together in his little sanctuary. Thomas was buried in the graveyard at St. Thomas Anglican Church.

By the late 20th century, the property was in bad shape. The roof had completely collapsed and only part of the walls were standing. The site was basically a hangout for the Island monkeys.

Thanks to the efforts of David Robinson, a work group from the Elderhostel Program came to Nevis and did a good job in partially restoring the little church making it a safe and attractive place to visit. In addition to the plaques on the walls of the building showing the names of the attendees, there is a small kiosk with informative bulletins which describe the history of the church and the restoration process.

In addition to frequent visits by locals and visitors alike, the site has become a popular place for weddings.

Eva Wilkin was born in the British Colony of Montserrat, about fifty miles Northeast of Nevis.

Her grandparents were from the UK. She came to Nevis with her parents and her sister. Her sister married a Mr. Maynard but had no children. Mr. & Mrs. Maynard moved to St. Kitts where Mr. Maynard was appointed manager of the sugar factory.

As Eva got older, she developed a love for painting. Miss Wilkin never married. Painting was the love of her life. She had local employees, a housemaid and a gardener who cared for her large garden. Eva painted portaits of her workers. She was one of the best artists on the Sister Islands for her time.

I knew Miss Wilkin and her sister and brother-in-law, Mr. Maynard. He was a very tall white fellow whose great grandparents were plantation owners when sugar was king on Nevis.

When the Maynards retired, they returned to Nevis to live at the Great House with Eva. Even when she was an old lady, in her eighties, she still painted until she could no longer carry on.

Mr. Maynard died at the age of 91 as did his wife and Eva as well. It was strange that all three died at the same age. When Eva passed, her paintings soared in value. I have been most impressed by the painting of the maid who worked for her for more than fifty years.

Eva Wilkin's work was promoted through the dedication of Howard and Marlene Pain.

They purchased her property and opened a gallery which not only had paintings and prints done by Eva, but also regular showings of works by other artists most often with Nevisian themes. Both Howard and Marlene as well as Dottie Burton and John and Barbara McFarland have captured Nevisian traditions and scenery in their art. The Pains worked hard to keep the property in great shape, not only the gallery, but also the Great House and the surrounding gardens.

The gallery was in a sugar mill which had been kept in great shape though it was built several centuries ago. It was a charming place for locals and visitors to peruse the artwork displayed there and to take a journey back in time.

The Nevis Triathlon, started by Winston Crooke who runs a business called Cycle World at Oualie Beach, has been a boost to the Nevisian economy in that it brings racers and their friends and families from all over the world who stay at our hotels, eat at our restaurants and consume our goods and services.

The day of the race, there is a need for a substantial number of volunteers sometimes numbering more than fifty and including both locals and visitors. They help out in many ways such as operating kayaks to help swimmers in distress, passing out water on bike and running courses, marking racers with their entry number and in general helping to steer racers in the proper direction.

Recruiting and coordinating the volunteers requires considerable effort.

After many years in this role, Paula and Don Flemming turned over the reins to David and Maureen Ferg who have continued to keep the ball rolling.

Bob Muroff, a man of many talents, gives up many hours to teach Nevisian youngsters to swim. I think this is important since we live on an island—we all should know how to swim. Bob started a program to give kids swimming and surfboarding lessons. Obviously, you must be able to swim in order to surf as you often fall off the board. Bob has been sharing his skills with Nevisian kids for years thus contributing to the well-being of our people.

Marie Clark had a small art gallery near the foot of Craddock Road. She displayed the work of local artists and worked hard to promote their work. She was especially interested in Nevisian painter, Margaret Fraser. Marie had a one-woman show to promote Margaret's work, one that proved quite successful as Margaret's paintings now hang in many homes on the Island.

The Foster family came to Nevis in the mid-sixties to build the Zetlands Hotel. They brought with them their young son, Seth. As Seth grew up, he began working with his father doing construction work.

Zetlands Hotel was built on Pond Hill with great views of Montserrat and Antigua/Barbuda. It was a charming place, much like Cliff Dwellers.

Guests at each hotel would visit the other one for lunch or dinner from time to time. The Fosters were great hosts as well as easy-going people. They were much loved by Nevisians.

After many years on Nevis, the Fosters returned to the US as they were getting on in age. Their son, Seth, continued to visit Nevis with his family, first for a few weeks and then following retirement, for the whole winter. The Fosters have played an important role in improving the standard of living on Nevis. The Island is a better place because of these folks who have done so much to help our people.

Barbara Whitman started a program called "Under the Sea". It was housed at Oualie Beach and was a sort of hands-on aquarium. Barbara would bring children in to get a close-up look at sea creatures of all types. She wanted to make them not only more knowledgeable but also more respectful of the life of the sea.

Bill and Stella Nokes, from Western Canada, first visited St. Kitts and Nevis back in November, 1963, around the time that President Kennedy lost his life, assassinated, so they say, by Lee Harvey Oswald on November 22. The Nokes visited both Islands and while they liked them both, they chose Nevis as the place to invest in real estate.

When they first came to Nevis, their two sons were quite small, maybe one and a half and three. Stella, who is larger than life, is a very kind lady. Her husband, Bill, supports her 100% in everything she does.

They have frequent visitors from abroad including friends and family, and often entertain their friends among the "expats" here on Nevis.

I should point out that most of the folks we Nevisians call "expats" are not really expatriates but rather "snowbirds" who come to enjoy our pleasant climate while escaping snow and ice in the frozen North.

Stella will liven up any party with her anecdotes and antics. There is never a dull moment when she's around. Bill is fast on the linguistic draw always looking for a punny way to get a laugh.

The Nokes have worked to keep the young men on Nevis out of trouble. They have contributed to ARK (Animal Rescue and Kindness) and have made donations to the local Red Cross and the Alexandra Hospital.

For many years, Ted Cox grew pineapples and grapefruit at his place in Churchground which he marketed at local stores. In spite of his constant struggles with the monkeys, he proved to local farmers that Nevis can overcome its dependency on other islands to supply us with fresh produce. As an architect, he helped with several projects on the Island. His wife, Barbara, taught many folks, both locals and expats, to play bridge.

Janet Cotton and her Aunt came to Nevis in the early seventies. They loved the ocean and would go out to sea together many times. Janet owned a house in Jones Estate which she called "Yellow Shutters". The house still stands today.

When Janet was off Island—she was just in her early fifties and still working in the US, she would rent her house to guests.

Janet was a kind and loving American who gave a lot to charity including the local Red Cross and the home for the elderly which in the old days, we called the "Poor House" because only those folks who were very old and unable to feed themselves were housed there. The Government put them up as they had no means of support.

Janet and her Aunt not only contributed money but they also brought materials from the US to assist in the care of the elderly.

One day, some thirty-two years ago, Janet and her Aunt took off in their rubber dinghy to go for a sail. Janet and her Aunt went missing and no word was heard from or about them.

The weather was a little rough that day and their boat was quite small. In any case, they never made it back to Nevis. A Coast Guard cutter was anchored off the bay at Oualie Beach. It left in search of the missing women but called off the effort after several days with no results. There was not a sign of them anywhere. They were great people and we miss them a lot.

Stuart Charles Smith and his wife, Jane, came to Nevis in the late sixties to vacation at the Cliff Dwellers Hotel. They fell in love with Nevis and bought property in Jones Estate.

Some time later, they hired the Cliff Dwellers' contractor to build them a home. It was a large three bedroom house with four underground cisterns. In those days, water was hard to come by. During the dry season, you would get very little running water. Three of their cisterns were filled by rain water. The fourth was used for grey water that came from the showers and the kitchen sink.

The property consisted of an acre and a half of land. The house was of concrete block construction with a bright red tiled roof. As a result, Stuart came to be called "Red Roof Smith".

During the early years of their ownership of the property, the Smiths never had a gardener. Both were still working up in Rochester, New York. They had two children, Stuart, Jr. and Carey. Carey was a very pretty young lady who went on to be a teacher.

I knew the family very well as I used to visit them when they came to Nevis. In 1976, the Smiths asked me to take care of the property and to plant a garden for them. The first thing I did was to fence in the property because there were lots of stray animals roaming around Jones Estate. So I landscaped the property and put in a lot of fruit trees including mango, pineapple, sugar apple, grapefruit, orange, lime. I also planted a lot of flowers and palm trees that are still there.

In 1977, the Smiths retired and began to spend winters on Nevis. Mrs. Smith would bring her elderly mother down from time to time depending on how she was feeling.

By 1980, Jane Smith's mother was not doing well as her health was failing. Stuart decided to sell the house and move back to the States. They moved from Rochester, New York, to North Carolina. In the winter of 1981, they sold their house on Nevis to Rod Pendergast whom I worked for for a short while.

Mark Schroeder, a retired engineer from Connecticut, for many years tutored students from the Gingerland area in Math and other subjects thus enabling them to be successful in their studies.

Jim Johnson came to Nevis about twenty-five years ago as a Peace Corps volunteer and fell in love with Nevis. After his service ended, Jim stayed on Nevis and started a business taking groups on bird-watching excursions as well as hikes to places of interest on the Island.

Jim married a local woman and had two children. In addition to giving tours to visitors, both resident and shipboard, Jim did a lot of work in the local schools.

Jim took many hikers to Nevis Peak and to the water source above Golden Rock. Though he was from the US, Jim knew the mountain and its trails better than most Nevisians. Jim also worked to preserve both our natural history and our archeological sites.

Some years ago, Jim died when his house went up in flames in the middle of the night. Although the authorities announced there was no evidence of foul play, many folks believe that Jim's life was wrongly taken by those who had a grudge against him.

In any case, his death was a big loss for Nevis and his contributions should be acknowledged and long remembered.

Don Mills came to Nevis from the US to retire. Some time later he discovered that a Canadian from Quebec had started up a hydroponic lettuce business on Westbury Road. This man was getting tired of working the business and his health was not so good so Don and a friend decided to take over the business.

The farm still produces the best lettuce on Nevis, and the business has expanded to produce other salad greens as well as cut flowers. Don is very dedicated to the business. When he is called, he will deliver the produce wherever. He even takes produce to the ferry and sends it to customers in St. Kitts. Don's business services all the hotels and restaurants on Nevis.

Don has created employment for Nevisians and is teaching them to grow hydroponic lettuce. In keeping with his generous nature, Don regularly supports local charities.

The Hallstrom family from Fern Hill has made significant contributions to Nevis. Diane has been instrumental in the work of the Animal Rescue Committee. Harry maintains a weather station and his reports are used not only by individuals but by official weather stations in the Caribbean.

He also maintains a reporting service to record crimes—mostly break-ins—which occur on Nevis. He does this in order to maintain a police and public awareness of the problem in hopes that some action might be taken.

Several years ago, Wayne and Charmaine Bossola came on vacation to Nevis. They loved the Island and its people and soon they were involved with animal rescue and caring for stray animals on Nevis.

They were also concerned about our young people who were getting into trouble. So they got to know some of our children and encouraged them to stay in school to get a good education. Furthermore they were concerned about the health care on Nevis. So they went to the Alexandra Hospital to see how they could help. They bought some equipment and other materials for the hospital so that the Nevisians could receive better health care.

I must also mention that Canada gave Nevis two schools in 1970. One was the St. Thomas Parish School.

Before that, we had the St. Thomas Church School which operated by the Anglicans for more than a hundred years. The Church School grew to serve over five hundred children. We were packed in tight! Most of us had classes outside on the grounds because space was so limited. When the Canadian Government decided to give us a new school, it was a great relief.

Every Wednesday, the children had to go up to St. Thomas Church for a one hour service.

It was intended to be food for our young souls. The teachers had to go as well. Most of the years I spent at St. Thomas School, the Reverend Eake from the UK was the parish priest.

In those days, we would receive lots of powdered milk from Canada, and once a week all the children would get a warm glass of milk.

I had four different Principals while I was at St. Thomas School. In my day, we called them Head Teacher. If you arrived at school late and the Head Teacher was in a bad mood, you would get a whipping.

Headmaster Elliot spent two years at St. Thomas School after which he was transferred to New River all-age school.

Next was Miss Roveter Butler from Charlestown. She was my favorite Principal. I never got a whipping from her. Many of the children loved her because if you had a good excuse for being late, you would not get a beating.

After she moved on to Gingerland, there was Miss Sylvia Byron who was also from Charlestown. She had the longest tenure at St. Thomas. She was a good educator but quick to use the strap. Her father was a shoemaker so she got leather straps from him. She didn't use them sparingly! Nobody wanted to come in contact with Miss Byron. She would come down heavy with the leather on your back. Sometimes she would make children lie on a bench to get a beating.

I was glad when she was transferred to New River after Mr. Elliot drowned on the MV Christena. It went down in the summer of 1970. Mr. Elliot lost his son in the same disaster. Following Miss Byron we had Mrs. Violet Nicholls. She became Headmistress the September after the new school, built by the Canadians, was opened. She was the first Head Teacher of the new school.

I left the school soon after that, so I didn't really have much contact with her. I know she was a lovely person and coincidentally, my second cousin. She went on to become Senior Education Officer on Nevis, a position she held until she retired from a long career—about forty years—in education. She continued to tutor children free of cost after retiring.

The Iva Walters Primary School was also a gift from the Canadian Government. The School is located in St. John Parish. It used to be called the Prospect School but was renamed in honor of a long-serving principal.

Mr. Walters was a teacher who always went the extra mile to educate the children at that school. Even when he was the Head Teacher, he would go into classrooms to teach the children and let them know that education was their key to a better future.

Mr. Walters is no longer with us today, but his legacy lives on as many of our young people turn out to be educators themselves.

The Methodist Church in Nevis also created two schools to educate our children.

One was in Charlestown High which served only boys. The Anglican School educated the girls. Both schools were at that time all-age schools. Children would start at five years of age and continue until they were sixteen. At that point, if they passed a standardized test, they could go on to Charlestown High School. The children in Gingerland attended High School there. Nowadays, everyone moves on to highschool at twelve years of age.

I must say THANK YOU on behalf of all Nevisians to our friends from the United States, Canada and around the world who have done so much for us. You have made the Island what it is today. Because of your contributions to Nevis, the Island is moving in the right direction.

You came here to retire because of your love for our Island and its people. But you saw both needs and opportunities and you responded wholeheartedly to both. You have created a healthy private sector, and our people now have a much higher standard of living because of you. We sincerely hope that you will continue doing all you do.

Much love to you all,
Ozzie
Oswald "Ozzie" Tyson

Made in the USA
Charleston, SC
12 January 2015